THIS JOURNAL IS DEDICATED
IN LOVING MEMORY OF:

_____

INTRODUCTION

I'm sorry. I didn't want us to meet this way. If you're reading this journal, I know you have experienced some loss and still are in the healing process. Thank you for finding this journal and using it as the first step to healing through grief. I am grateful that you chose this journal as a resource to start your journey. This road is not easy, but you will get through it.

I want to tell you that I understand. I know you have heard this one million times, but I know your pain. The crumbling of your heart when you found out, the denial, the anger, the depression — it seems so hard to believe. And I know, it feels so unfair.

I came up with the idea for a grief journal a few weeks ago. I lost my grandparents, Dennis Lindsey and Deborah Carroll, in 2009 and 2011, back to back. Nothing could have prepared me for losing my grandparents. They were both only 58, and I was 18 and 21 at the time. I talked to a friend experiencing grief this week, and I broke down. It's been almost ten years, and there are so many things I wish I could tell them, and this is how I came up with *Things I Wish I Could Tell My Angels*.

You are not alone. It gets better. You feel the weight of grief on your shoulders. I know that some days it feels like you are drowning. Sometimes you can be perfectly okay and then start crying in the middle of nowhere. You do not feel okay. My hope is that each day feels a little lighter; each day feels a little brighter until you are finally back to yourself.

Your friend,
India Lindsey

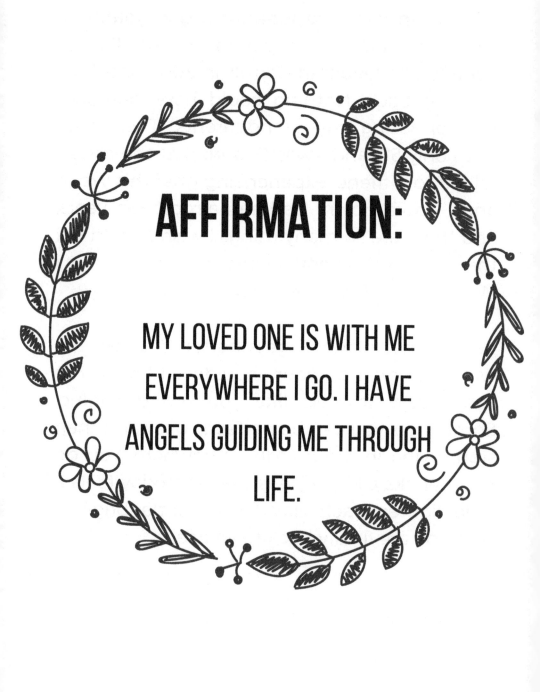

AFFIRMATION:

MY LOVED ONE IS WITH ME
EVERYWHERE I GO. I HAVE
ANGELS GUIDING ME THROUGH
LIFE.

THIS IS MY FAVORITE PHOTO OF US:

my loved ones favorites:

color: _____

book: _____

song: _____

food: _____

holiday: _____

flower: _____

drink: _____

movie: _____

activity: _____

tv show: _____

THIS IS MY FAVORITE PHOTO MY LOVED ONE:

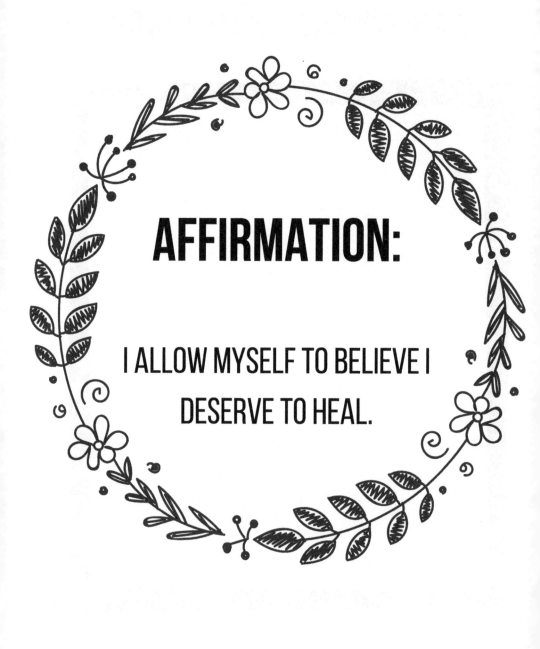

AFFIRMATION:

I ALLOW MYSELF TO BELIEVE I
DESERVE TO HEAL.

Daily Mood
TRACKER

DATE		M	T	W	R	F	S	S

HAPPY	DEPRESSED	MOODY	ANGRY
JOYFUL	SAD	LAZY	FEARFUL
CALM	LONELY	OKAY	ANXIOUS
RELAXED	MOODY	PRODUCTIVE	ANNOYED
CONTENT	EXHAUSTED	FRUSTRATED	MAD AS HELL

WHAT WENT WELL: _____

_____

_____

_____

COULD BE BETTER: _____

_____

_____

_____

reflection

THERAPY NOTES

MY MOOD:

HOW THINGS WENT THIS WEEK:

IMPORTANT THINGS TO REMEMBER:

HOMEWORK:

reflection

_____

_____

_____

_____

_____

_____

_____

_____

_____

_____

_____

_____

_____

_____

Daily Mood
TRACKER

DATE		M	T	W	R	F	S	S

HAPPY	DEPRESSED	MOODY	ANGRY
JOYFUL	SAD	LAZY	FEARFUL
CALM	LONELY	OKAY	ANXIOUS
RELAXED	MOODY	PRODUCTIVE	ANNOYED
CONTENT	EXHAUSTED	FRUSTRATED	MAD AS HELL

WHAT WENT WELL: _____

_____

_____

_____

COULD BE BETTER: _____

_____

_____

_____

reflection

Daily Mood
TRACKER

DATE		M	T	W	R	F	S	S

HAPPY	DEPRESSED	MOODY	ANGRY
JOYFUL	SAD	LAZY	FEARFUL
CALM	LONELY	OKAY	ANXIOUS
RELAXED	MOODY	PRODUCTIVE	ANNOYED
CONTENT	EXHAUSTED	FRUSTRATED	MAD AS HELL

WHAT WENT WELL: _____

_____

_____

_____

COULD BE BETTER: _____

_____

_____

_____

THERAPY NOTES

MY MOOD:

HOW THINGS WENT THIS WEEK:

IMPORTANT THINGS TO REMEMBER:

HOMEWORK:

AFFIRMATION:

I ACCEPT WHAT I CANNOT
CHANGE AND FIND THE COURAGE
TO CHANGE THE THINGS I CAN

Daily Mood
TRACKER

DATE		M	T	W	R	F	S	S

HAPPY	DEPRESSED	MOODY	ANGRY
JOYFUL	SAD	LAZY	FEARFUL
CALM	LONELY	OKAY	ANXIOUS
RELAXED	MOODY	PRODUCTIVE	ANNOYED
CONTENT	EXHAUSTED	FRUSTRATED	MAD AS HELL

WHAT WENT WELL: _____

_____

_____

_____

COULD BE BETTER: _____

_____

_____

_____

reflection

AFFIRMATION:

I FOCUS ON MY BLESSINGS,
GOALS, AND MEMORIES.

Daily Mood
TRACKER

DATE		M	T	W	R	F	S	S

HAPPY	DEPRESSED	MOODY	ANGRY
JOYFUL	SAD	LAZY	FEARFUL
CALM	LONELY	OKAY	ANXIOUS
RELAXED	MOODY	PRODUCTIVE	ANNOYED
CONTENT	EXHAUSTED	FRUSTRATED	MAD AS HELL

WHAT WENT WELL: _____

_____

_____

_____

COULD BE BETTER: _____

_____

_____

_____

reflection

_____

_____

_____

_____

_____

_____

_____

_____

_____

_____

_____

_____

_____

_____

THERAPY NOTES

MY MOOD:

HOW THINGS WENT THIS WEEK:

IMPORTANT THINGS TO REMEMBER:

HOMEWORK:

AFFIRMATION:

IT'S OKAY TO TAKE TIME TO
GRIEVE.

Daily Mood
TRACKER

DATE	M	T	W	R	F	S	S

HAPPY	DEPRESSED	MOODY	ANGRY
JOYFUL	SAD	LAZY	FEARFUL
CALM	LONELY	OKAY	ANXIOUS
RELAXED	MOODY	PRODUCTIVE	ANNOYED
CONTENT	EXHAUSTED	FRUSTRATED	MAD AS HELL

WHAT WENT WELL: _____

_____

_____

_____

COULD BE BETTER: _____

_____

_____

_____

reflection

THERAPY NOTES

MY MOOD:

HOW THINGS WENT THIS WEEK:

IMPORTANT THINGS TO REMEMBER:

HOMEWORK:

AFFIRMATION:

I AM THANKFUL FOR THE TIME I
SHARED WITH MY LOVED ONE.

Daily Mood
TRACKER

DATE		M	T	W	R	F	S	S

HAPPY	DEPRESSED	MOODY	ANGRY
JOYFUL	SAD	LAZY	FEARFUL
CALM	LONELY	OKAY	ANXIOUS
RELAXED	MOODY	PRODUCTIVE	ANNOYED
CONTENT	EXHAUSTED	FRUSTRATED	MAD AS HELL

WHAT WENT WELL: _____

_____

_____

_____

COULD BE BETTER: _____

_____

_____

_____

reflection

_____

_____

_____

_____

_____

_____

_____

_____

_____

_____

_____

_____

_____

_____

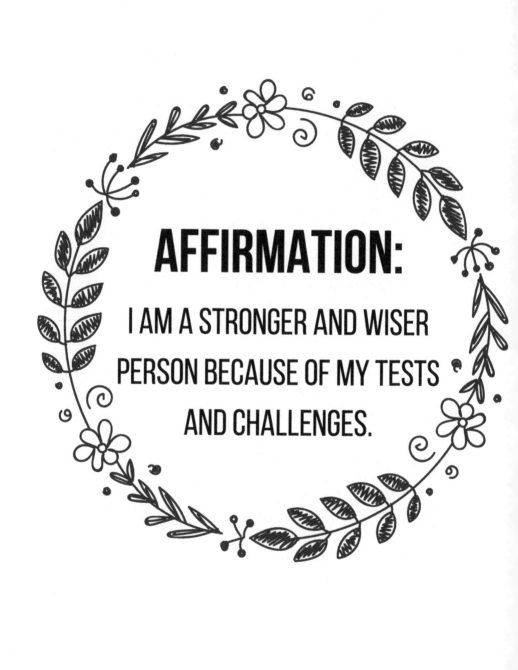

AFFIRMATION:

I AM A STRONGER AND WISER PERSON BECAUSE OF MY TESTS AND CHALLENGES.

reflection

Daily Mood
TRACKER

DATE		M	T	W	R	F	S	S

HAPPY	DEPRESSED	MOODY	ANGRY
JOYFUL	SAD	LAZY	FEARFUL
CALM	LONELY	OKAY	ANXIOUS
RELAXED	MOODY	PRODUCTIVE	ANNOYED
CONTENT	EXHAUSTED	FRUSTRATED	MAD AS HELL

WHAT WENT WELL: _____

_____

_____

_____

COULD BE BETTER: _____

_____

_____

_____

THERAPY NOTES

MY MOOD:

HOW THINGS WENT THIS WEEK:

IMPORTANT THINGS TO REMEMBER:

HOMEWORK:

AFFIRMATION:

I AM ABLE TO SEE THE GOOD IN MYSELF.

Daily Mood
TRACKER

DATE	M	T	W	R	F	S	S

HAPPY	DEPRESSED	MOODY	ANGRY
JOYFUL	SAD	LAZY	FEARFUL
CALM	LONELY	OKAY	ANXIOUS
RELAXED	MOODY	PRODUCTIVE	ANNOYED
CONTENT	EXHAUSTED	FRUSTRATED	MAD AS HELL

WHAT WENT WELL: _____

_____

_____

_____

COULD BE BETTER: _____

_____

_____

_____

reflection

THERAPY NOTES

MY MOOD:

HOW THINGS WENT THIS WEEK:

IMPORTANT THINGS TO REMEMBER:

HOMEWORK:

Daily Mood
TRACKER

DATE	M T W R F S S

HAPPY	DEPRESSED	MOODY	ANGRY
JOYFUL	SAD	LAZY	FEARFUL
CALM	LONELY	OKAY	ANXIOUS
RELAXED	MOODY	PRODUCTIVE	ANNOYED
CONTENT	EXHAUSTED	FRUSTRATED	MAD AS HELL

WHAT WENT WELL: _____

_____

_____

_____

COULD BE BETTER: _____

_____

_____

_____

reflection

_____

_____

_____

_____

_____

_____

_____

_____

_____

_____

_____

_____

_____

_____

AFFIRMATION:

I FOCUS ON MY BLESSINGS,
GOALS, AND MEMORIES.

Daily Mood
TRACKER

DATE		M	T	W	R	F	S	S

HAPPY	DEPRESSED	MOODY	ANGRY
JOYFUL	SAD	LAZY	FEARFUL
CALM	LONELY	OKAY	ANXIOUS
RELAXED	MOODY	PRODUCTIVE	ANNOYED
CONTENT	EXHAUSTED	FRUSTRATED	MAD AS HELL

WHAT WENT WELL: _____

_____

_____

_____

COULD BE BETTER: _____

_____

_____

_____

reflection

THERAPY NOTES

MY MOOD:

HOW THINGS WENT THIS WEEK:

IMPORTANT THINGS TO REMEMBER:

HOMEWORK:

reflection

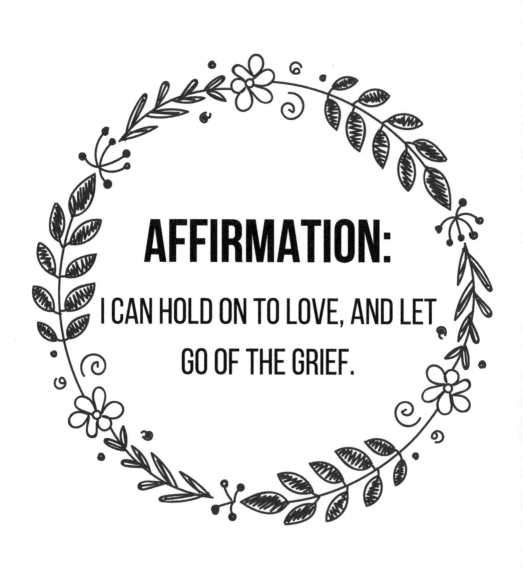

AFFIRMATION:

I CAN HOLD ON TO LOVE, AND LET

GO OF THE GRIEF.

Daily Mood
TRACKER

DATE		M	T	W	R	F	S	S

HAPPY	DEPRESSED	MOODY	ANGRY
JOYFUL	SAD	LAZY	FEARFUL
CALM	LONELY	OKAY	ANXIOUS
RELAXED	MOODY	PRODUCTIVE	ANNOYED
CONTENT	EXHAUSTED	FRUSTRATED	MAD AS HELL

WHAT WENT WELL: _____

_____

_____

_____

COULD BE BETTER: _____

_____

_____

_____

reflection

_____
_____
_____
_____
_____
_____
_____
_____
_____
_____
_____
_____
_____

AFFIRMATION:

I CHOOSE TO HEAL MY HURT
SPIRIT.

Daily Mood
TRACKER

DATE		M	T	W	R	F	S	S

HAPPY	DEPRESSED	MOODY	ANGRY
JOYFUL	SAD	LAZY	FEARFUL
CALM	LONELY	OKAY	ANXIOUS
RELAXED	MOODY	PRODUCTIVE	ANNOYED
CONTENT	EXHAUSTED	FRUSTRATED	MAD AS HELL

WHAT WENT WELL: _____

_____

_____

_____

COULD BE BETTER: _____

_____

_____

_____

reflection

_____

_____

_____

_____

_____

_____

_____

_____

_____

_____

_____

_____

_____

_____

THERAPY NOTES

MY MOOD:

HOW THINGS WENT THIS WEEK:

IMPORTANT THINGS TO REMEMBER:

HOMEWORK:

reflection

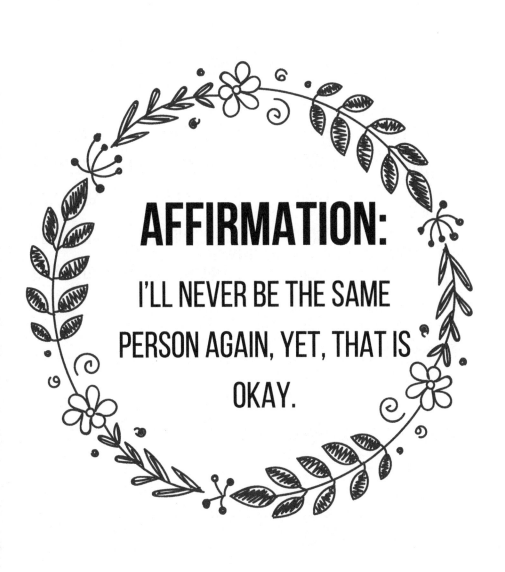

AFFIRMATION:

I'LL NEVER BE THE SAME
PERSON AGAIN, YET, THAT IS
OKAY.

Daily Mood
TRACKER

DATE	M	T	W	R	F	S	S

HAPPY	DEPRESSED	MOODY	ANGRY
JOYFUL	SAD	LAZY	FEARFUL
CALM	LONELY	OKAY	ANXIOUS
RELAXED	MOODY	PRODUCTIVE	ANNOYED
CONTENT	EXHAUSTED	FRUSTRATED	MAD AS HELL

WHAT WENT WELL: _____

_____

_____

_____

COULD BE BETTER: _____

_____

_____

_____

reflection

_____

_____

_____

_____

_____

_____

_____

_____

_____

_____

_____

_____

_____

Daily Mood
TRACKER

DATE		M	T	W	R	F	S	S

HAPPY	DEPRESSED	MOODY	ANGRY
JOYFUL	SAD	LAZY	FEARFUL
CALM	LONELY	OKAY	ANXIOUS
RELAXED	MOODY	PRODUCTIVE	ANNOYED
CONTENT	EXHAUSTED	FRUSTRATED	MAD AS HELL

WHAT WENT WELL: _____

_____

_____

_____

COULD BE BETTER: _____

_____

_____

_____

reflection

THERAPY NOTES

MY MOOD:

HOW THINGS WENT THIS WEEK:

IMPORTANT THINGS TO REMEMBER:

HOMEWORK:

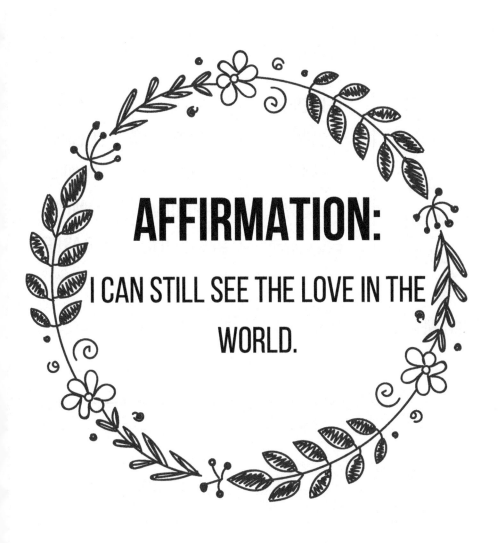

AFFIRMATION:

I CAN STILL SEE THE LOVE IN THE WORLD.

Daily Mood
TRACKER

DATE		M	T	W	R	F	S	S

HAPPY	DEPRESSED	MOODY	ANGRY
JOYFUL	SAD	LAZY	FEARFUL
CALM	LONELY	OKAY	ANXIOUS
RELAXED	MOODY	PRODUCTIVE	ANNOYED
CONTENT	EXHAUSTED	FRUSTRATED	MAD AS HELL

WHAT WENT WELL: _____

_____

_____

_____

COULD BE BETTER: _____

_____

_____

_____

reflection

_____

_____

_____

_____

_____

_____

_____

_____

_____

_____

_____

_____

_____

_____

THERAPY NOTES

MY MOOD:

HOW THINGS WENT THIS WEEK:

IMPORTANT THINGS TO REMEMBER:

HOMEWORK:

AFFIRMATION:

TODAY, I CHOOSE TO HEAL.

Daily Mood
TRACKER

DATE		M	T	W	R	F	S	S

HAPPY	DEPRESSED	MOODY	ANGRY
JOYFUL	SAD	LAZY	FEARFUL
CALM	LONELY	OKAY	ANXIOUS
RELAXED	MOODY	PRODUCTIVE	ANNOYED
CONTENT	EXHAUSTED	FRUSTRATED	MAD AS HELL

WHAT WENT WELL: _____

_____

_____

_____

COULD BE BETTER: _____

_____

_____

_____

reflection

_____

_____

_____

_____

_____

_____

_____

_____

_____

_____

_____

_____

_____

_____

reflection

_____

_____

_____

_____

_____

_____

_____

_____

_____

_____

_____

_____

_____

THERAPY NOTES

MY MOOD:

HOW THINGS WENT THIS WEEK:

IMPORTANT THINGS TO REMEMBER:

HOMEWORK:

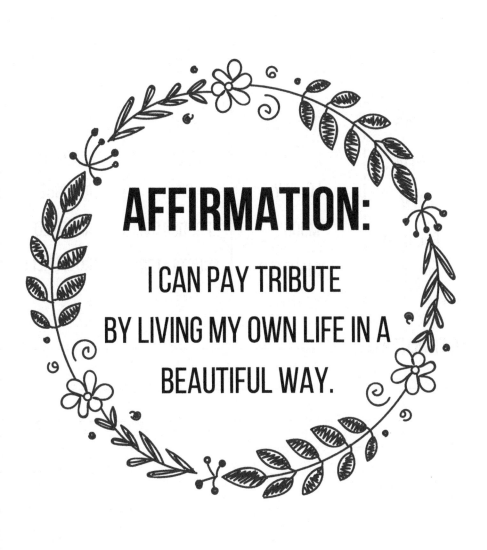

AFFIRMATION:

I CAN PAY TRIBUTE
BY LIVING MY OWN LIFE IN A
BEAUTIFUL WAY.

Daily Mood
TRACKER

DATE		M	T	W	R	F	S	S

HAPPY	DEPRESSED	MOODY	ANGRY
JOYFUL	SAD	LAZY	FEARFUL
CALM	LONELY	OKAY	ANXIOUS
RELAXED	MOODY	PRODUCTIVE	ANNOYED
CONTENT	EXHAUSTED	FRUSTRATED	MAD AS HELL

WHAT WENT WELL: _____

_____

_____

_____

COULD BE BETTER: _____

_____

_____

_____

reflection

_____

_____

_____

_____

_____

_____

_____

_____

_____

_____

_____

_____

_____

_____

_____

_____

Daily Mood
TRACKER

DATE		M	T	W	R	F	S	S

HAPPY	DEPRESSED	MOODY	ANGRY
JOYFUL	SAD	LAZY	FEARFUL
CALM	LONELY	OKAY	ANXIOUS
RELAXED	MOODY	PRODUCTIVE	ANNOYED
CONTENT	EXHAUSTED	FRUSTRATED	MAD AS HELL

WHAT WENT WELL: _____

_____

_____

_____

COULD BE BETTER: _____

_____

_____

_____

reflection

_____

_____

_____

_____

_____

_____

_____

_____

_____

_____

_____

_____

_____

_____

Daily Mood
TRACKER

DATE		M T W R F S S

HAPPY	DEPRESSED	MOODY	ANGRY
JOYFUL	SAD	LAZY	FEARFUL
CALM	LONELY	OKAY	ANXIOUS
RELAXED	MOODY	PRODUCTIVE	ANNOYED
CONTENT	EXHAUSTED	FRUSTRATED	MAD AS HELL

WHAT WENT WELL: _____

_____

_____

_____

COULD BE BETTER: _____

_____

_____

_____

reflection

_____

_____

_____

_____

_____

_____

_____

_____

_____

_____

_____

_____

_____

THERAPY NOTES

MY MOOD:

HOW THINGS WENT THIS WEEK:

IMPORTANT THINGS TO REMEMBER:

HOMEWORK:

MEMORIES

Made in the USA
Las Vegas, NV
02 December 2020